BY THE
Word
MOMENTS

A DEVOTIONAL GUIDE

LINDA M. THOMPSON

Published By:
Jasher Press & Co.
customerservice@jasherpress.com
1.888.220.2068
New Bern, NC 28561

Copyright© 2016
Interior Text Design by Pamela Simmons
Cover Design by Pamela Simmons

ISBN: 978-0692687420

First Edition
Printed and bound in the United States of America

BY THE

Word

MOMENTS

A DEVOTIONAL GUIDE

I dedicate this book to my family but most of all, the Lord Jesus Christ who is the author and finisher of my faith. Through him I am inspired to live by the Word.

INTRODUCTION

IF you're reading this introduction that means you either purchased the book, received it as a gift or you're reading it in the store. However you may have received this book, let me say thank you for taking the time to allow me to invade your world. I must say I never thought in a million years that I would be one of the millions of individuals who write books but what can I say, God truly works in mysterious ways.

My writing started early one morning. I woke up and found myself thinking about my crazy life. I could not believe where I was and how I got there. And just like that I turned on the computer and began to type away as I heard the voice of God speak to me. The first passage described one of those light-bulb moments in my life when I discovered the purpose for my greatest hell.

You see in 2008 I became a widow. Early one Sunday morning I received one of the worst messages of my life from the local police officer. My husband of 20 years died in his sleep from an epileptic seizure while he was out of town. I was now that widow that you read about in all of those books and watch on all the Lifetime movies with two teenage daughters to rear alone.

However God would not allow me to have a pity party no matter how bad I wanted to send out the invitations and bake those pity cookies. He had the nerve to drive me to His Word. The more I became angry about my situation the more He reminded me of my predecessors who experienced similar grief, pain and disappointment. When I wanted to sink in my grief He reminded me of Mary the mother of Jesus. When I tried to die in my disappointment and loneliness and He took me to the pit where Joseph laid helpless at the bottom only to be sold into slavery by his brothers. He reminded me of Joseph's words "But as for you, ye thought evil against me; but God meant it unto good, to bring to pass, as it is this day, to save much people, alive. (Genesis 50:20)" Yes I thought the death of my husband was sent to harm me. It took me a while to realize that it was part of God's plan to bring me and my husband to an expected end. You see it's easy to forget when you're grieving that death is a part of life and we must all die one day. The problem is no one wants to die or wants to say good-bye so we endure the harsh pain of grief and wonder how we will survive in the end.

God eventually helped me to realize that my husbands' death was a part of my life's process. Just like the pit, the prison and the palace was a part of Joseph's. I realized after 20 years of marriage that God's focus for my marriage wasn't the house, two kids, a wonderful career, status or money. God simply wanted our love for each other to be so strong that it would push us right into the arms of Jesus. The best thing I could do as a wife was to cover my husband with the love of Jesus by encouraging him to live a life for God. As we both loved and lived for God our ultimate destination would be with Christ. Now eight years later I am blessed because God has restored my joy by blessing me to marry again. I now realize that marriage isn't about what I get, it's about what I give.

By the Word Moments is a 52 week devotional guide inspired by God to help you explore the Word and way of God throughout your year. At the end of each devotion you will find a light bulb note – take time to think about each one as you meditate on this devotion throughout the week. Make notes and make your own light bulb remarks, you'll be blessed by how God speaks to you. I pray they will bless you as much as they have blessed me.

COSTUME JEWELRY

I recently started wearing costume jewelry. Never really took an interest in it before, but the fancy colors and designs really began to catch my eye. I like it so much that I've started carrying a line in the bookstore I manage. There is this one bracelet that I really love to wear; I wear it just about every day. A few days ago I noticed some red discoloration on the metal part of the bracelet. I later learned that it turned that color because of the oils in my skin. I also realized that because the bracelet was not made of a precious authentic metal like silver or gold it wasn't going to stay the same. Wow! My life was once like that bracelet, it looked great on the outside, but the more I lived it begun to turn. That's because my life wasn't real without Jesus. The moment I accepted him and began to wear his authentic Word, my life became purer and more genuine. Now when I wear my bracelet I don't worry about the discoloration because it simply reminds me that I serve an authentic GOD!

People who are often plagued with low self-esteem find themselves trying to match up to others so called perfect lives. Remember God's grace transformed us to be better in His sight. Jesus Christ' approval is the only one that matters and He gave us His seal of approval at Calvary. "And every man that hath this hope in him purifieth himself, even as he is pure. (1 John 3:3)"

LIGHT BULB MOMENT:

Think about your personal imperfections and write a list of about 5 or so. After you finish ask God if He cares about them. Write down God's response to you. I'm wondering if His response to you is the same response He gave to me.

_____
_____
_____
_____
_____
_____
_____
_____
_____
_____
_____
_____
_____
_____
_____
_____
_____
_____
_____
_____
_____
_____
_____
_____
_____
_____
_____
_____

Week 2

PATIENT PARKING

Have you ever been in a hurry and trying to find a parking space, only to get behind a slow driver who seemed to be browsing, passing every space and taking their precious time? I recently went to the mall and found myself behind a very slow driver. They actually passed several parking spaces, driving at a snail's pace. Finally I passed them and swerved into a parking space. Frustrated and impatient at the driver, **I later noticed them pulling into a handicapped space.** Wow! I really felt bad when I saw the couple exit the car and the driver was actually using a cane. How could I have been so impatient and not willing to think about the driver of the car's needs instead of mine? I wanted to exit the car and apologize but instead I just asked God to forgive me for my selfish frustration.

Aren't you glad God isn't impatient with us? He walks with us and talks with us no matter how long it takes us to get where we're going. He doesn't swerve past us, or even roll his eyes. I'm reminded of the scripture in 2 Peter 3:9, "The Lord is not slack concerning his promise, as some men count slackness; but is longsuffering to us-ward, not willing that nay should perish, but that all should come to repentance." Thank God for life's patient parking and the ability to get it right the next time I'm in the parking lot of life.

Light Bulb Moment:

Write down five things that get you easily frustrated. After you list each one, write down how God would respond to each one of them. It's amazing how our little idiosyncrasies are just that little in the sight of God.

Five Frustrations

1.

2.

3.

4.

5.

Week 3

JUST GO GET IT

During my morning meditation I had a chance to read Matthew 21:2-3. I chose this scripture because it outlined the events leading up to the triumphal entry of Jesus Christ. This is what it says, "Go into the village that is over against you, and straightway ye shall find an ass tied, and a colt with her: loose them, and bring them unto me. 3And if anyone say aught unto you, ye shall say, The Lord hath need of them; and straightway he will send them."

What amazed me about these two little powerful verses was the wealth of wisdom they contained. Firstly, Christ commanded his disciples to go get two animals that didn't even belong to them. I wonder how they felt about going onto someone else's property and doing what they may have considered to be robbery. Imagine during these times people were put to death for stealing, in some cases their hands were cut-off. But not only did He ask them to do such a risky task, He also told them what to say if questioned by the owner and lastly He reassured them by saying, "he will send them".

How many times has the Holy Spirit commanded you to do something that you thought was ridiculous, only to later find out that **God had already made provision for the vision?** Think about it, each time He tells us what to say and assures us that everything is going to be alright. Slowly but surely I'm learning that my obedience to God even in the most trying times yields the greatest rewards. **I can't tell you how many times I've come to realize that what I thought was unthinkable, God took and made**

possible all for my good. So today I've decided to go get it! Everything that the Holy Spirit has commanded me to get I'm going to get it!!!

LIGHT BULB MOMENT:

Name something that God has told you to pursue and because of doubt you thought it was unthinkable.

_____
_____
_____
_____
_____
_____
_____
_____
_____
_____
_____
_____
_____
_____
_____
_____
_____
_____
_____
_____
_____
_____

Meditate on this scripture for the week:
Ephesians 3:20 " Now unto him that is able to do exceeding abundantly above all that we ask or think, according to the power that worketh in us." **Now go get it!**

Week 4

CHANGING LANES

I recently took my oldest daughter to an Open House at a local college she's thinking about attending. On the road trip I became a little misty reminiscing on the past 18 years with my beautiful baby and now she has blossomed into this amazing young woman. All of sudden I quickly crept up on this slow moving vehicle and I had to change lanes. Later in the week I realized no matter how much I reminisced about her childhood and the wonderful memories I've come to cherish, **we are now at a point in both of our lives that we must change lanes.** And while the mother in me wants to keep a tight hold on my beautiful child, the God in me realizes that it is all a part of God's plan.

That's how it is with God, no matter what the past holds, our future directs us to move over into a new lane of life where we find ourselves speeding beyond our pasts and moving quickly towards a new and bright future. Paul reminds us in 2 Corinthians 5:17 "Therefore if any man be in Christ, he is a new creature: old things are passed away; behold all things are become new." I'm grateful for the memories, the baby pictures, the visions of her joyful childhood, but I'm even more excited to see her evolve into a mature and willing servant in the Body of Christ. Thank you God for allowing me to put on my signal and gracefully move over into the lane of life you've ordained for me and my family.

LIGHT BULB MOMENT:

It's hard sometimes to let go of the past but the new memories that you can make with Jesus Christ are more than you could ever dream about. List a moment from your past that keeps holding you back.

_____
_____
_____
_____
_____
_____
_____
_____
_____
_____
_____
_____
_____
_____
_____
_____
_____
_____
_____
_____
_____

Father in the name of Jesus I ask you to remove the strongholds in my life and those things that keep me from moving closer to you and realizing my destiny with you. In Jesus name AMEN! Now change lanes!

CREATURE OF HABIT

My morning devotions seem to change each day as I approach God. No one morning seems the same. One morning I may lay prostrate before Him, another morning I may move and stretch in His presence, this morning I simply read. At first it bothered me because I wanted to make sure my devotion was pleasing to God. However He reminded me that anytime I include Him in my day and acknowledge Him in all of my ways, He is pleased. When I acknowledge Him, the Holy Spirit will lead and guide me into all truths. No longer are my decisions based on my carnal knowledge, but on Godly wisdom.

While God never changes--we do! And while our human nature is to become creatures of habit, we must realize when we take on the mind of Christ we are new creatures, 2 Corinthian 5:17 says "Therefore if any man [be] in Christ, [he is] a new creature: old things are passed away; behold, all things are become new. " That means me and you. We are new in Christ Jesus, that also means every day with Jesus is new. Aren't you glad He doesn't bring up the past; he simply teaches us to move forward and allows the old to pass away? So the next time I rise for devotion I will look forward to seeing what new thing God and I can do together. The most important thing is that I include Him in my day. **Thank God I am not a creature of habit; I am a new creation in Jesus Christ!**

LIGHT BULB MOMENT:

Describe one of your devotional experiences with God. Is it the same experience each day? Or do you change your approach to God?

_____

_____

_____

_____

_____

_____

_____

_____

_____

_____

_____

_____

_____

_____

_____

_____

_____

_____

_____

_____

_____

_____

_____

_____

Remember God is excited every time you include Him in on your day!

PIDDLIN WITH JESUS

"Piddlin" according to my mother, grandmother and a lot of aunties, means to stir about the house completing light household chores – dusting and moving papers from place to place, wiping down walls, just little things. However "Piddlin" has a special spiritual connection for us, when the women in my family piddle they traditionally hum Christian hymns or speak to the Lord quietly while moving about. "Piddlin" for me has become something special, passed down from one generation to the next. In the beginning I thought my mom and aunts were kind of weird when I heard them doing this … and now look who's picked up the family tradition. My daughters see and hear me when I piddle, I see them smile like I did and whisper among themselves. Oh, how I'd love to be a fly on the wall and listen to what they have to say.

It was during one of my morning "Piddlin" sessions that I began to hum an old revised hymn I hadn't heard in more than 15 years. "Jesus Saves"… The opening lines reads, "We have heard the joyful sound, Jesus saves, Jesus saves, spread the tidings all around, Jesus saves, Jesus saves. To the utmost Jesus saves, to the utmost Jesus saves, he will pick you up and turn you around Hallelujah, Jesus saves. Right in the midst of my "Piddlin" everything stopped and I began to thank God for saving me and picking me up, turning me around and changing my whole life. **I began to thank God for saving me from everything that could have consumed me.** For the next few minutes my house changed from a cleaning spot to a sanctuary where God received my undivided attention. I wonder if we all piddled a little more what would happen in our homes. Would our houses become cleaner? Would our children see us differently and would God receive more glory from our praise and devotion? I say yes to all of the above. Give it a try, put "Piddlin" on your daily calendar and watch God move.

LIGHT BULB MOMENT:

Well here's your chance to get it in, while doing some light house work start to hum a favorite hymn or praise song. Meditate on the words of the song and watch God move house-work to worship.

_____
_____
_____
_____
_____
_____
_____
_____
_____
_____
_____
_____
_____
_____
_____
_____
_____
_____
_____
_____

Week 7

THE PERFECT PARENT

As I moved past the Mother's Day holiday, I had an even greater appreciation for my mother this year. At the age of 77 years old her body is now in need of a tune-up. A recent surgery has left her limited and now needing the full and undivided attention of her children. My sisters and I are honored to serve my mother during this difficult time in her life and ours. And while it is visibly obvious that she is still in charge… the smile on her face shows that she's glad we are there and listening to every word. Each day I enter her room with anticipation to her every request wondering how I can make her day better than the day before. Why? Because I love her and nothing is more important to me than seeing my mother happy and fulfilled.

David reminded me in Psalms 116: 1-2 that God is also attentive to me, this is what it says –"I love the Lord, because he hath heard my voice and my supplications. Because he hath inclined his ear unto me, therefore will I call upon Him as long as I live." There's joy in knowing that God recognizes my voice from everyone else. He doesn't clump me in a pile and bless me just like everyone else. God knows my name, He knows my voice and He is drawn to me. He knows my every situation, my every circumstance and He cares. And when God listens I know and anticipate that He will always show up and come to my rescue. Why because He loves me. So I've decided to be like David, I've made up my mind that I will call upon Him as long as I live.

LIGHT BULB MOMENT:

How often do you call upon God? Do you think that you are bothersome with your requests? God loves to hear from you. Remember--**don't allow your requests to outweigh your praise!** As you rise each day to complete your devotion list five things God has done for you that morning and consider how God has proven to be the perfect parent in your life.

_____

_____

_____

_____

_____

_____

_____

_____

_____

_____

_____

_____

_____

_____

_____

_____

_____

_____

_____

_____

_____

_____

_____

_____

_____

MORNING PERSON

While traveling away on business, I woke early one morning and began my morning devotion. I thanked God for allowing me to see another day. When I went down to the hotel lobby for breakfast, there was a woman sitting near-by at another table, who seemed to be melting with joy. She was on her cell phone having a loud and exciting conversation. She was smiling, she was laughing all at 7:30 in the morning. I looked around the room to see if I was the only one annoyed by this. However no one else was there. I tried to continue reading the newspaper for the day however she kept talking and laughing. Annoyed I went to the coffee stand and prepared my shot of caffeine for the day. The server looked at me and asked this question politely, "that coffee will help you start your day want it?"

Immediately I realized that this picture was all wrong. I had forgotten just that quickly about my devotion. I forgot just that quickly, that it wasn't the coffee, the soft bed, the breakfast or even the alarm clock that allowed me to start my day--it was Jesus! I found myself taking on the familiar mind-set that so many of us take on...I'm not a morning person, when in fact I really was. You see when God allowed me to wake up that morning that meant I was a morning person, an afternoon person, an evening person and a midnight person. Why? Jesus intended this for me. David put it very simply, Psalms 118: 24 "This [is] the day [which] the LORD hath made; we will rejoice and be glad in it." Notice he didn't break the day down into parts he simply embraced the entire day and decreed that he would rejoice in it, because God created it. So from this point on I am a morning person... The entire day has been set before me and I will rejoice in it, because if God allowed me to see this day, He intended for me to treasure every second of it.

LIGHT BULB MOMENT:

 COME ON AND WAKE UP it's a great day to rejoice. As you rise to another wonderful week of devotion learn to appreciate the sunshine and all of God's beautiful creation. Each day this week as you review this devotion think about God's first days upon the earth as outlined in Genesis 1:1-31. Consider how He embraced each day with purpose. Now consider how you will embrace each day this week with purpose and authority.

WHERE ARE YOU FROM?

It's a common part of our greeting; people want to know where you're from when they meet you for the first time. Most folks are interested because they want to see if they're familiar with the place. Unfortunately many folks have a tendency to pre-judge us based on where we live. It happens all the time we judge people based on their status in life, the neighborhood they live in, the school they went to, the church they attend or simply how they look.

I wonder how Jesus felt when Nathanael judged Him? Nathanael said in John 1:46," Can anything good come out of Nazareth?" The implication was that nothing powerful or awesome could ever come from this community. You see Nazareth was a small farm village with about 1500 people living in it during Jesus' time. No one famous or prosperous had come from Nazareth. As a matter of fact rumor had it that this man named Jesus was a fraud. How many times have people pre-judged you? They judged you based on your appearance, based on rumors, your size, your shape, your hair, the way you speak, where you live, the way your home looks. They even judge you based on your family.

But Jesus approached Nathanael and identified him on the spot, however he didn't judge Nathanael based on his hometown or even his outward appearance he revealed to Nathanael the truth, who he really was and where He had seen him. He told Nathanael I saw you under the fig tree before Phillip called you. Jesus sees us before anyone else does. He knows who we are and where we are in this journey called life. Jesus sees you. So the next time you want to know where someone is from, think of Nazareth and remember **don't judge them, just love them right where they are.**

LIGHT BULB MOMENT:

As you approach this week consider your greetings and introductions to individuals. Work on seeing the good in people instead of the negative. When you approach individuals this week begin to think of good things you can purposely say to each person.

Philipians 4:8 "Finally, brethren, whatsoever things are true, whatsoever things are honest, whatsoever things are just, whatsoever things are pure, whatsoever things are lovely, whatsoever things are of good report; if there be any virtue, and if there be any praise, think on these things."

BUSY-BODY

In years past I had to submit to an annual employee evaluation. My boss used a check-list and reviewed my areas of success and areas where I needed improvement. I noticed the busier I was the better my evaluation was. The more programs and initiatives I had the better the evaluation. I was very pleased because a good evaluation meant a raise was somewhere in my future. Overall I was a good employee, and I always excelled above and beyond on my evaluations. It was what I had come to expect.

That started me to thinking about my work history with Jesus. I wondered what He would write if He had to evaluate my work. I wondered if I would pass the check-list of righteous living. And while I know He loves me and forgives me for all of my wrongs, I can't help but wonder if I'm doing ok. I recently began studying about Mary & Martha, the two sisters who had a sincere desire to serve and please Jesus, but they went about it in different ways. Martha was busy in her approach to service and Mary served while at the feet of Jesus.

Then I remembered the scripture where Martha approached Jesus about her work. I can only imagine that Martha thought she would receive a good evaluation. This is what she said, "Lord, dost thou not care that my sister did leave me to serve alone? Bid her therefore that she help me. 41But the Lord answered and said unto her, Martha, Martha, thou art anxious and troubled about many things: 42but one thing is needful: for Mary hath chosen the good part, which shall not be taken away from her."

I now realize that I don't want to be so busy that I forget that Jesus is The Boss and I can't do anything without His divine instruction. So I must acknowledge Him first. I must come into His presence give Him my undivided attention and He will give me wisdom and instruction in my service. So now instead of worrying about my evaluation with Jesus, I have made up my mind before I get busy "in all my ways I'm going to acknowledge him and He will direct my path. (Proverbs 3:6)"

LIGHT BULB MOMENT:

As you plan your week take time out to ask God for his divine instruction on how to make this week a time of purpose and blessing. Be busy with a divine purpose. Write out God's instructions for you this week.

_____
_____
_____
_____
_____
_____
_____
_____
_____
_____
_____
_____
_____
_____
_____
_____
_____
_____
_____

MINE IS BIG TOO

I recently found myself worrying about bills. Yes I must admit after all the shouting and praying there are times when my mind becomes overwhelmed with the responsibilities of life. In the midst of my humanness I take a pause and ask God how this is going to end. But when I turn on the news and look at the tragedies across the world, the deaths, destruction and sadness I realize if I put my problems on a scale with everyone else's my problems aren't so bad after all. That's when I felt kind of convicted for worrying in the first place. After all I had food, shelter and a reasonable portion of health as the ole folk say.

But the Holy Spirit reminded me that in the eyes of God all of our problems are BIG and deserve all of his attention. You see God reminded me that we are the ones who put problems on this scale of 1-10. He doesn't, He has compassion for us whether we're at a 1 or at a 10. I'm reminded of the story of Jairus in the book of Mark the 5th chapter. He approaches Jesus pleading with him to come see his daughter who was at the point of death. While Jesus proceeded to Jairus' house, the crowd pressed against him. In this crowd there was a woman who had been bleeding internally for 12 years.

She pressed through the crowd and in faith touched the hem of Jesus' robe. The bible tells us that she was healed immediately. I love this part, because Jesus didn't just keep moving, He didn't say, you're a "5" and this little girl is a "10." He stopped right where she was and acknowledged her faith and ministered to her and told her that her faith had made her well. Moments later He proceeded to Jairus' house to find that the little girl had died. I realized from this that what we think is over--is never really over! It's not too little or too late in the eyes of Jesus. Jesus proceeded to the house and raised the little girl from the dead.

I've decided this morning to throw away my scale, and to cast all of my cares upon him for he cares for me! And while I pray for the crisis of this world, I'll remember that while my God is BIG, He's never too big to come and see about little ole me.

LIGHT BULB MOMENT:

How often do we dismiss other people's problems? Take this week to examine the problems of others. Ask God to resolve their problems with the same urgency that you use and watch God move on their behalf.

_____
_____
_____
_____
_____
_____
_____
_____
_____
_____
_____
_____
_____
_____
_____

Week 12

TRIP OR JOURNEY

While visiting with my mom one afternoon we began to talk about life and the choices we make. Her words of wisdom were so inspiring, but there was something that she said that I'll never forget. That afternoon my mother told me, "Life with Jesus is a journey; not a trip. You can't stop whenever you want to. You must follow His directions." I was simply amazed by this powerful nugget. I soon realized that much of my struggles on this road to righteousness came when I tried to make a stop along the way and Jesus had not ordained it. You see there were times when I wanted to lay down and simply get off the road and go in another direction. I wanted to cuss someone out, I wanted to make decisions based on my own intellect, I wanted to do it my way. That's when the struggle began; my spirit man was in battle with the spirits of this world. You see the world had shown me that if I do it this way it will work, however I had to soon realize that Jesus really does know best.

Psalms 24:1 reads, "The earth is Jehovah's, and the fulness thereof; The world, and they that dwell therein." If this earth really belongs to Him then He must know better than anyone what will work. So I've decided to stay on this journey called life, I've decided to be a passenger with Jesus and follow His directions. No matter how hard it may seem, no matter how long it may take, He has everything I need to make the journey. That means when I get hungry along the way, He'll feed me, when I'm tired He'll allow me to rest, when I need to make a stop, He'll lead and direct me—after all He's the one driving.

LIGHT BULB MOMENT:

GPS or Jesus! The next time you get in a car think about how important directions are. Without them we would truly be lost. Thank God for divine instructions this week. He is our heavenly navigator on this road called life.

_____
_____
_____
_____
_____
_____
_____
_____
_____
_____
_____
_____
_____
_____
_____
_____
_____
_____
_____
_____
_____
_____
_____
_____
_____
_____
_____

Week 13

HOSPITALS – A PLACE OF SURRENDER

I have a new respect for hospitals and for those who work in them. After spending several days and nights along my mother's side during her temporary illness, I felt somewhat helpless because laying my hands or applying the anointing oil didn't make everything alright instantly. I had to sit back and allow God and the medical staff to do their work. And while I know that God heard my prayers and the prayers of many others as always, there was nothing left to do but wait.

God had allowed the hospital to become the perfect place of surrender for me. No longer could I depend on my skills, intelligence or even who I knew, He simply wanted me to move out of the way and allow Him to do what He promised - heal my mother. In Matthew 11:29-30 Jesus had this to say, "Take my yoke upon you, and learn of me; for I am meek and lowly in heart: and ye shall find rest unto your souls. 30For my yoke is easy, and my burden is light." A yoke is a wooden frame that fits over the shoulders of large animals, banding them to each other and to the plow they pull together. To be yoked to Christ means to rely on Him, to give Him our burdens, and to accept the necessity of walking with Him, side by side.

When I decided to yoke up with Jesus on this situation and to hand my burdens of worry, frustration, helplessness and fear over to Him; I was no longer worried or frustrated. The situation became lighter. Why? Because Jesus doesn't worry, He isn't afraid, He is a present help in the time of troubles. **Today I'm glad that Jesus has an**

exchange policy! I encourage you to exchange your cares for His because He cares for you.

LIGHT BULB MOMENT:

Think about all the burdens you carry around. Take an opportunity to make a list this week and each day try to release one of them over to God. I promise you--you will feel much better.

_____
_____
_____
_____
_____
_____
_____
_____
_____
_____
_____
_____
_____
_____
_____
_____
_____
_____
_____
_____
_____
_____
_____
_____
_____
_____

Week 14

CASTING YOUR BREAD UPON THE WATER

Have you ever wondered what God thinks about the economy and the way we handle business today? I have! As a matter of fact I recently read a scripture in the book of Ecclesiastes that helped me to understand that God wants us to make big investments. Ecclesiastes 11:1-2 reads, "Cast thy bread upon the waters; for thou shalt find it after many days. 2. Give a portion to seven, yea, even unto eight; for thou knowest not what evil shall be upon the earth."

King Solomon wrote this passage and in it he wanted to encourage the believer to act with faith that the benefit of their good deeds will not be lost. That means he wants us to invest in each other and unlike many who follow the stock market with payouts as their motives for investing. God doesn't want us to stand around waiting on our return. Rather God wants us to exercise our faith. God wants our motives to be pure and sincere.

In these days of worldly uncertainty man has lost his ability to simply trust God and step out on faith. However those of us who know the Word and trust in God with all of our hearts should always be willing to invest in others. That means even when our funds are at their lowest we should be willing to cast our bread and whatever else we have to others. If they're hungry feed them, if they're naked clothe them, if they're homeless find them a place to sleep. If they are burdened down encourage them. Make an investment every day. The return may not be immediate but when it does arrive it will be greater than you could ever imagine!

LIGHT BULB MOMENT:

Consider investing in someone this week. Ask God to send someone in need of help your way and watch God bless you to be a blessing.

_____
_____
_____
_____
_____
_____
_____
_____
_____
_____
_____
_____
_____
_____
_____
_____
_____
_____
_____
_____
_____
_____
_____
_____
_____
_____
_____
_____
_____

A FATHER'S WISDOM

As we approach this Father's Day it's hard to believe but I have joined the ranks of those whose fathers are now resting with the Lord. In 2001 just one month prior to the World Trade Center attack my father passed away suddenly. While his memory is larger than life I appreciate his loud and echoing voice more and more. He would say things like family is the most important thing in the world. You should always help somebody out. And yes, my favorite saying was "Get somewhere and sit down." I was always trying to figure out why I had to go somewhere, why couldn't I just sit down.

My father pastured for more than 50 years. He loved people and he took the word of God seriously and he really tried to follow the letter of the law. I remember when I was very young I heard my father preach about Abraham and Isaac. I remember him preaching how obedient Abraham was when he took Isaac on the mountain to offer him as a sacrifice to God. His loud rumbling voice shouted to the congregation the importance of obeying God's word. While the story ended with God providing another sacrifice instead of Isaac. I was afraid for months after that sermon that my father was going to lead me up on a mountain top and offer me to God and depending on how bad I had been that month, there may not have been a sacrifice hiding in the bushes.

I learned later from my father, that I no longer had to worry about being that sacrifice that God had already sent the perfect sacrifice for me and that was his son Jesus. Proverbs 4:1 reads, "Hear ye children, the instruction of a father, and attend to know understanding." I pray that you will appreciate the wisdom of your father or a father-like figure in your life and embrace them with love and honor.

LIGHT BULB MOMENT:

Take a moment to reflect on the father figures in your life, write down some of the important lessons they've shared with you. Now take time to tell them thanks.

_____
_____
_____
_____
_____
_____
_____
_____
_____
_____
_____
_____
_____
_____
_____
_____
_____
_____
_____
_____
_____

YOU CAN NEVER THANK TOO MUCH

Have you ever asked God for something big and just as He promised He gave you what you asked for? How long did you thank God before you started asking for something else? I heard a preacher explain that our appreciation should last longer than our request. That started me to thinking about the number of times I really show God my appreciation during the day and how many times I make requests. There are days when I know that my requests certainly out number my thanks.

Then I thought about King David - while David was a man after God's own heart it was evident that David had moments of joy, sadness and depression. Throughout much of Psalms we see David making requests and then a few chapters over he praises God. Listen to David in Psalms 17:6-9. It reads, "I pray to you, O God, because you answer me; so turn to me and listen to my words. 7 Reveal your wonderful love and save me; at your side I am safe from my enemies. 8 Protect me as you would your very eyes; hide me in the shadow of your wings 9 from the attacks of the wicked. Deadly enemies surround me."

Now listen to Psalms 18: 1-2 the song written after David was rescued. It reads, "2 The Lord is my rock and my fortress and my deliverer, my God, my rock, in whom I take refuge, my shield, and the horn of my salvation, my stronghold. 3 I call upon the Lord, who is worthy to be praised, and I am saved from my enemies." Throughout most of the Psalms we find David and others making many request, followed by royal praises.

God is our father and He certainly wants his children to be blessed. However the next time you make a request of God, remember to allow your appreciation to outlast your petition. The best way to do this is by thanking God in advance. Yes, before your request, in the middle of your request and after it, God deserves our praises in season and out of it.

LIGHT BULB MOMENT:

During your devotion this week take time to thank God for each blessing. You will probably have a difficult time remembering them all so just thank Him for everything. Before each prayer thank Him for what He's already done. This should become a daily part of your devotion.

_____
_____
_____
_____
_____
_____
_____
_____
_____
_____
_____
_____
_____
_____
_____
_____
_____
_____
_____

DAILY BREAD

Ever wonder why God doesn't give us all of our blessings in one big package and send us on our way? Ever wonder why He doesn't just let us hit the lottery? While that sounds great and would certainly solve many of my current problems, I realize it won't solve the big problem and that is simply learning to trust God with my daily portion. Matthew 6:11 reads, "Give us this day our daily bread". This prayer taught by Jesus indicates that the bread "manna" that God provides for us daily is more than enough to get us to the next day. The question I have to ask myself is what am I doing with the daily bread He gives me? And can I be trusted with more of this manna from heaven?

The Children of Israel had a problem trusting God with their daily portion. Remember in the book of Exodus when God rained down manna from heaven. Each person was instructed to take only their individual portion. The scripture tells us that those who took too much had nothing left over and those who took the allotted amount had no lack. Those who fell into greed and tried to gather for the next day awakened to find their food spoiled. When we are greedy and unappreciative of our daily portion we adopt a spirit of waste and over indulgence.

I'm asking God to help me enjoy my daily portion, to make me a good steward over my manna. I'm forgetting about the meal for tomorrow and thanking him and blessing him for today's portion. God wants to know if He can trust me with this daily portion before he can increase what He gives me. Ask yourself can God trust me with more?

Matthew 25:21 reads "thou hast been faithful over a few things, I will make thee ruler over many things: enter thou into the joy of thy lord."

LIGHT BULB MOMENT:

Here's your chance to get rid of waste from your life. Make a list of the things you waste each day. During this week ask God to make you a good steward over your blessings. Now find ways to use your blessings wisely. Enjoy your manna!

_____

_____

_____

_____

_____

_____

_____

_____

_____

_____

_____

_____

_____

_____

_____

_____

_____

_____

_____

_____

_____

_____

_____

_____

Week 18

Holy Temple

For the past few mornings I've been praying for healing among many family members and friends. While praying I began to wonder about my own temple and what kind of physical shape I'm really in. I began to take a personal inventory of how I eat, drink, exercise and rest. While my inventory didn't yield the best results, I realize that there is so much more that I should be doing to make sure that my body is holy and acceptable unto God.

I'm reminded in Romans 12:1 that Paul pleaded with the church to present their bodies as living sacrifices, holy and acceptable unto God. And while Paul's request centered around loyalty and dedication to service, it also pleaded with us to present our very best to God. This means we must take care of our bodies. When you board a plane the flight attendant takes a few moments before lift-off to review emergency landing instructions with each passenger. One of the instructions to parents is that when air pressure is lost in the cabin, oxygen masks will automatically fall from the ceiling of the plane. The flight attendant instructs parents to apply their oxygen mask first and then apply it to your child. The first time I heard this it sounded a little ridiculous, but then I realized that if I wasn't breathing, I couldn't help my child. I had to put my health and wellness first in order to be of service.

If my body isn't acceptable then I can't do the work that God has commanded of me. If I'm sick all the time, tired, sad, or depressed, then my body is not in acceptable condition to do service. How many of us have neglected our bodies and are unable to provide the service that God's people need? Don't let your service to God be hindered because of neglect and self indulgence. Join with me today as I declare and decree to present my body holy and acceptable unto God, which is my reasonable service. I will love my temple the way God loved it when he made me.

LIGHT BULB MOMENT:

Now is the time to take a personal inventory of your eating and exercise plan. Write down what you eat and the type of exercise you do for five days. Now examine what's on your list. Can you improve? If so begin working slowly to changing your eating patterns and your exercise plans. Now watch as God will help you to create a temple worth the worship.

_____
_____
_____
_____
_____
_____
_____
_____
_____
_____
_____
_____
_____
_____
_____
_____
_____
_____
_____
_____
_____
_____
_____
_____
_____

Week 19

I LEAVE WORK AT THE OFFICE

I heard someone say the other day that when they leave work that they leave work at the office and don't take it home. They were inferring that they leave all the mess and stresses of the work-place at the office. However I discovered that while we think we leave it at work we really don't. While you may not talk about work at home or the people you work with, our actions, attitudes and the stresses of the workplace are often reflected in how we interact with our family and friends. That can sometimes cause problems in the home when we don't take the time to pray about our work day.

Imagine working in a slaughterhouse, smelling like the stench of hogs. When you finished working you didn't shower or even bother to change your clothes. You just got in your car, drove down the road and entered your home. Your family has now been exposed to your work. And while you didn't bother to discuss your time at work or even talk about the little piglets, your family received the horrible aroma of the slaughterhouse. You took your work home. It happens daily in your home and mine. We don't realize how the pressures of work can spill over into our personal lives. However God has as remedy for this--It's called prayer.

Prayer helps to clean us up. It helps us to wash away the stresses and strains of our daily lives so we don't infect those we love by our bitterness and mood swings. Philippians 4:6-7 reads, "Don't worry about anything, but in everything, through prayer and petition with thanksgiving let your requests be made known to God.

7 And the peace of God, which surpasses every thought, will guard your hearts and your minds in Christ Jesus." So the next time you have a stressful day at the office remember to say a little prayer. Ask God to wash away the smell of your daily pressures, so your family and loved ones won't have to endure the aroma.

LIGHT BULB MOMENT:

Now that you're working towards washing away the daily stresses of the job, start your time after work by asking your family members to share their day first. Consider the wonderful things that happened and thank God for them. Now take a few minutes to review your day and ask God to show you the good in spite of the bad.

_____
_____
_____
_____
_____
_____
_____
_____
_____
_____
_____
_____
_____
_____
_____
_____
_____
_____
_____
_____

Week 20

COMFORTABLE PEWS

Growing up in ministry I have had the pleasure of sitting on church pews most of my life. From the cushion-less hard oak pews of the old church furnishings to the modern day cushioned pews that provide the ultimate comfort during church services. Church pews were designed to provide maximum seating for large groups of people. However during my life-time I've never seen a pew praise God. The pews like the seats in your home provide a place for the body to rest, however our spirits should find comfort and joy seated in the presence of the Lord. The bible tells us that in the presence of the Lord there is fullness of joy.

Worshipping God is an active experience. Throughout the book of Psalms the believer is commanded to praise Him with the dance, with a song, with the instruments – the believer is encouraged to rejoice. The last Psalm; Psalm 150 ends by saying Let everything that has breathe praise ye the Lord, Praise ye the Lord. And since I'm breathing and you're breathing, we should take every opportunity that God gives to release praises in the atmosphere. **That means I have an obligation as a believer not to allow my spirit to become lazy but to show God how much I love him with my praise.**

Now for everyone praise is different, for some praise is loud and busy. For others praise is quiet and calm. However you choose to praise God make sure it's your best. Make sure you give God all you can, when you can. David says in Psalms 145:2-3, "Every day will I bless thee; and I will praise thy name forever and ever. Great is the

Lord and greatly to be praised; and his greatness is unsearchable." David decided to praise God everyday based on what he had done for him. I've decided to join David and praise God every day.

LIGHT BULB MOMENT:

Take the time this day to praise God without prompting. I guarantee you that you will feel much better!

_____
_____
_____
_____
_____
_____
_____
_____
_____
_____
_____
_____
_____
_____
_____
_____
_____
_____
_____
_____
_____
_____

HOLD YOUR PEACE

I recently had a conversation with a friend about being lied on. And while we found ourselves quoting familiar scriptures and sounding deep and spiritual, we realized that being lied on really hurts. It causes some serious emotional scars and even some real tears. And while my spirit man is supposed to be big and strong, my earthly man wants to fight and yeah even cuss someone out.

During my daily devotion I ran across Matthew 10:17-19, that covers the instructions given by Jesus to the Disciples as he prepared to send them out. Jesus explains in this chapter that men will go to any lengths to discredit and cause you to fall. They will even take you before Governor's and kings. Here is what he says "But when they deliver you up take no thought how or what ye shall speak: for it shall be given you in that same hour what ye shall speak. For it is not ye that speak, but the Spirit of your Father which speaketh in you. Verse 22 reads "and ye shall be hated of all men for my names' sake, but he that endureth to the end shall be saved."

That helped me tremendously because it allowed me to understand that being lied on is part of my job as a believer. And while it doesn't feel good, I also realize when they're lying on me, they're really lying on Jesus and according to this scripture He will give me the words to say. Not the cuss words, not even allow me to put my hands on my sanctified hips and give them a piece of my mind. He will give me Godly wisdom and allow me to speak as He would speak. In other words this battle isn't mine, it's

His. And as usual my Savior, my Big Brother Jesus, wants to fight for me. So I've decided that while the tears may fall and I may get a little upset, I'll just let Jesus handle it. Because when Jesus handles it, it's finished.

LIGHT BULB MOMENT:

Create a job description for you as a believer. Write down five things that a believer must be willing to endure. Review the list and ask yourself how you're doing with the tasks. If you notice that you need to improve, then write down different ways that you can improve your endurance for Christ.

_____

_____

_____

_____

_____

_____

_____

_____

_____

_____

_____

_____

_____

_____

_____

_____

_____

_____

_____

_____

_____

_____

_____

Week 22

HE CHOSE US

Do you remember when you were growing up playing outside with your friends and then you decided to form a dodge ball team? That was the time when the draft truly began. I dreaded that time because I wasn't such a good player. Everyone was usually faster and kicked farther than I did. And so the dreaded draft often left me standing at the end with the kid that was just as bad as I was. The feeling that I wasn't good enough to be on anyone's team was awful. Especially when the team captains argued over who would get me and that wasn't because either side wanted me to play. I soon realized that dodge ball wasn't my game and that I should just sit on the sidelines and watch.

I'm glad today that Jesus chose me the moment I decided to play on his team. He didn't examine me to see what kind of player I would be, he didn't worry if I was quick enough or kicked far enough, he simply took me as I was and opened his arms for me to come running. In the book of Mark Jesus scolded the Disciples for trying to keep the little children from coming to Him. Mark 10: 14 – 16 reads, "But when Jesus saw [it], he was much displeased, and said unto them, Suffer the little children to come unto me, and forbid them not: for of such is the kingdom of God. Verily I say unto you, Whosoever shall not receive the kingdom of God as a little child, he shall not enter therein. And he took them up in his arms, put [his] hands upon them, and blessed them.

Regardless of how the world may leave me out and cast me to the side, I'm so glad that Jesus has enough love to take me in his arms and love me with all of my flaws. The next time you're feeling alone and left out, imagine Jesus holding you in His arms and showering you with blessings and love. Have a great day.

LIGHT BULB MOMENT:

Take this week to help lift someone's spirits who seems to always be on the sidelines. Start a conversation with them, let them know that you notice them and care. Your positive conversation can make them feel like a star!

_____
_____
_____
_____
_____
_____
_____
_____
_____
_____
_____
_____
_____
_____
_____
_____
_____
_____
_____
_____
_____
_____
_____
_____
_____

Week 23

BE DOERS OF THE WORD

I woke up early one Saturday morning to find that my schedule for the day was very full. I had a breakfast meeting, a speaking engagement and a business presentation. And right in the midst of my busy morning I received a phone call from someone needing my help. I immediately began to run down my schedule to them and outline my very busy and hectic day. Then I decided to find someone else to serve them. However there was no one there to help. And in just a few moments the Holy Spirit moved upon me in a still quiet thought and said, "you go".

I was reminded instantly that while my schedule was busy God's schedule is never busy; and while I have the chance to serve my brothers and sisters I should always avail myself to do the work of the Lord. You see, I really had the time needed to serve them. My afternoon was open; however I forgot just in an instance that in all of that busy work it was God's kingdom work that was the most important. It became easy for me to make excuses and convince myself that I was too busy to do anymore work.
James 1:22-25 reads, "Do not merely listen to the word, and so deceive yourselves. Do what it says. Anyone who listens to the word but does not do what it says is like a man who looks at his face in a mirror and, after looking at himself, goes away and immediately forgets what he looks like. But the man who looks intently into the perfect law that gives freedom, and continues to do this, not forgetting what he has heard, but doing it--he will be blessed in what he does."

My prayer today is, "God don't let me forget who I am and whose I am. I am your servant and I must remember that your work is the most important work. **Lord don't allow me to become so busy living life, that I forget to live the life that you have destined for me.** Forgive me for making excuses and help me to serve my fellow man without excuses and resentment, In Jesus Name AMEN.

LIGHT BULB MOMENT:

Take this week to offer your time and service to someone out of the ordinary. Inconvenience yourself for someone else. That's called being unselfish.

_____
_____
_____
_____
_____
_____
_____
_____
_____
_____
_____
_____
_____
_____
_____
_____
_____
_____
_____
_____
_____

Week 24

NEVER ALONE

During some of the windiest moments of hurricane Irene, I found myself feeling very helpless and alone. And while the storm for me wasn't as bad as some of the hurricanes I had endured; the howling wind that rattled my windows and shook the trees like toy sticks was un-nerving at times. That's when I found myself praying the most, when I felt helpless and alone.

In Psalms 91:11-14 David reminded me, that just when I thought I was alone, God had protectors watching over me 24/7. This is what David wrote, "For he will command his angels concerning you to guard you in all your ways; they will lift you up in their hands, so that you will not strike your foot against a stone. You will tread upon the lion and the cobra; you will trample the great lion and the serpent. "Because he loves me," says the LORD, "I will rescue him; I will protect him, for he acknowledges my name." Instantly I realized that I was not alone in my storm.

Imagine President Obama forgetting that he had the Secret Service. You might say that's impossible because you know that every president has Secret Service protection. You can see them wherever he goes. Well God reaffirmed this to me through this scripture that we as believers have our very own Secret Service protection. And while we may not see the angels he has assigned to us – watching over us and protecting us they are there. How do I know? Because I made it through the storm. Remember even Satan knows God has assigned angels to you. Satan reminded Jesus in the wilderness when he tried to tempt

Him. He himself reminded Jesus that God would give his angels charge over thee. And if the enemy knows it we should know it.

God thank you for assigning me Secret Service protection everyday! Thank you for helping me to see when I feel lonely, your angels of protection are hovering over me and never leaving me alone. AMEN. Have a great day!

LIGHT BULB MOMENT:

This is a great time to reflect on the number of times God has sent protection our way and rescued you. I guarantee you'll begin to smile and even praise God.

_____
_____
_____
_____
_____
_____
_____
_____
_____
_____
_____
_____
_____
_____
_____
_____
_____
_____
_____
_____

Week 25

HOW BIG IS HE?

One day while driving my mind began to focus on a problem I was having. I soon discovered that my casual thoughts were turning to worry. Right in the middle of my worrying I heard the Holy Spirit ask me this question "How Big is Your God?" While sitting at the traffic light waiting for it to turn green, my eyes quickly turned to the sky, the trees and the creation around me. I imagined moving across the sky and going higher and higher with no way to stop and finally it came to me just as the problem did. My God is bigger than any problem that I could ever face! He is the CREATOR of every good and perfect gift. My God spoke one day and created light upon the earth and on another day he divided the waters. WOW!

I soon realized that this problem that I was worrying about was like a grain of sand on the beach to God. And while I am precious to him, my worries will not shift the foundations of the earth or create animals or trees, they will only cause frown lines on my face and perhaps an ulcer in my stomach. So I decided before I exited my vehicle to give my worry over to God. I decided to do whatever the Lord told me to do and leave the rest up to him. 1 Peter 5:7 tells us to "Cast all your anxiety on him because he cares for you."

No longer will I limit God based on my problem. I will remember that my problems are small in the sight of God and all I have to do is ask and He will work through me and for me. God is limitless! He is Bigger than anything or anyone I could ever imagine! That's how Big my God is!

LIGHT BULB MOMENT:

Try this exercise: Lift your arms as high as they can go. If there is still room above them that means that there is still more God.

_____
_____
_____
_____
_____
_____
_____
_____
_____
_____
_____
_____
_____
_____
_____
_____
_____
_____
_____
_____
_____

LION CHASER

I'm reading a fascinating book by Mark Batterson titled, "In A Pit With A Lion on A Snowy Day!" The title alone will make you frown, however it's one of the best books I've read this year. Without giving too much of it away, it talks about a man in 2 Samuel that many of us probably have never heard of by the name of Benaiah. He was one of David's mightiest warriors. Among his accomplishments were killing two of Moabs mightiest warriors, a seven foot giant, and my favorite is when he chased a lion in the snow into a pit! Then he kills him without a weapon. WOW!!! Ladies this was a bad man.

But throughout the book I realized that no matter how crazy God's instructions may sound, no matter how outnumbered you may feel, how small and insignificant you seem; If God said do it--he will equip you with the strength, speed, knowledge, courage and wealth to do whatever you need to get it done. Isaiah 55:8 reads, "For my thoughts are not your thoughts, neither are your ways my ways," declares the LORD." God doesn't think like us, He has no fear, He's not broke. He doesn't get depressed and worry about what other people might say. He is God and He does whatever He wants to do.

After reading the first half of this book I've decided I want to be a lion chaser. I want to pursue the impossible! I'm no longer concerned about what people say about me. I want everything God has for me and sometimes this means going into unchartered territory. So what if I'm the first one to do it. I know that I won't be alone because my God is right there with me on the journey, running into every pit that I may face! And when I come out I'll be victorious! Why? Because I'm not alone and my faith is in God!

_____

_____

_____

_____

_____

_____

_____

_____

_____

_____

_____

_____

_____

_____

_____

_____

_____

_____

_____

_____

_____

_____

_____

_____

_____

LIGHT BULB MOMENT:

Join me today as we mount up for this spiritual safari and go after the lions of life and slay them. Declare it today--I am a lion chaser. Have a great day!

_____
_____
_____
_____
_____
_____
_____
_____
_____
_____
_____
_____
_____
_____
_____
_____
_____
_____
_____
_____
_____
_____
_____

I MADE IT!

This is probably one of the hardest devotions I've had to share, however after praying about it, the Holy Spirit told me to share it because it would bless someone. On September 14, 2011 I passed a milestone in my life. It was three years to the date that my husband of 20 years passed away. When I looked at the calendar on that day something happened to me that had never happened before. I realized that after all I had gone through--I MADE IT! I wasn't in a mental ward, I wasn't in jail, I wasn't in the hospital, living on the street, my children weren't sick, I wasn't hungry, depressed or hopeless. I realized in that short time that I MADE IT through another year and I'm still standing by the grace of God. WOW!!!

You see at the moment of losing my husband three years ago life stopped for me. It was as if there was nothing left to do but stop living but God said not so! John 10:10 reads, "The thief comes only to steal, kill and destroy; I have come that they may have life, and have it to the full." When we lose a loved one our emotions tell us to stop breathing and to stop feeling. Our emotions tell our minds, bodies and souls to stop living. **It is the intent of the enemy to kill us in our grief.** But I thank God for the Holy Spirit and how He keeps us, leads us and guides us to the truth and reminds us of the abundant life that lies ahead. And while it may be hard to understand today in the middle of your grief, remember you will get through it and look back and say like those who have lost loved ones before, "It was because God was on my side that I made it!"

LIGHT BULB MOMENT:

My prayer today for everyone who has lost a loved one is that you will hear the voice of God right where you are and know that you will get through it. Breathe, breathe, breathe and allow God's life flowing spirit fill you and give you the peace that passeth all understanding. AMEN. Have a blessed day!

_____
_____
_____
_____
_____
_____
_____
_____
_____
_____
_____
_____
_____
_____
_____
_____
_____
_____
_____
_____
_____

Week 28

PRACTICE MAKES PERFECT

Have you ever told yourself you were going to think before you spoke? Perhaps you even told yourself you would just listen and not open your mouth at all? Well I keep telling myself these things, but it always amazes me how I often fall short and end up opening my mouth and sometimes inserting my foot where it doesn't belong; only to return home feeling remorse or guilt for what I've said or possibly implied. I then find myself repenting and yes even apologizing to those I may have wronged.

That's when the Holy Spirit reminded me of King David. While David was certainly a man after God's own heart, his life was filled with divine processes that kept him running back to God and asking for his divine forgiveness. He kept practicing a life pleasing to God. This is what David had to say in Psalms 32:5, "Then I acknowledged my sin to you and did not cover up my iniquity. I said, "I will confess my transgressions to the LORD" and you forgave the guilt of my sin." David didn't make any excuses as he came clean with what he had done. **Not only did God forgive the sin, He took away the guilt of the sin.** I've discovered that it's not only the reminder that I've sinned, but the guilt that holds me responsible for committing the act. No longer can I blame anyone else for what I've done, but I now have to take full responsibility for my actions. And just when you thought it was over God shows up and says you are forgiven and He takes on the guilt of your sin leaving us another opportunity to keep practicing this Christian life. WOW!!! He is certainly amazing.

72

LIGHT BULB MOMENT:

Webster defines the word practice like this: To perform or work at repeatedly to become proficient. Practice the act. I thank God for the rehearsals of life and the blessed opportunity to get it right in the body of Christ. I praise God that when I fall short, "He is faithful and just to forgive us [our] sins, and to cleanse us from all unrighteousness (1 John 1:9)". I'm glad that practice makes perfect in Jesus Christ.

STAY THE COURSE

There are days when I find myself in the book of Philippians pressing toward the goal to win the prize for which God has called me! Then on the other hand there are days when I'm just glad I'm in the race. I work with a couple of gentlemen who have become avid distance runners. Each day weather permitting they use their lunch breaks to suit up and hit the road for their 3 mile run. When they first started out I noticed they ran a short distance, slowly jogging along the road for only a few laps. Now a few months later their capable of running three miles and sometimes more. One of the young men just completed a marathon. He didn't realize it but I was just as happy as he was.

Now notice, I'm watching them from a distance observing their progress. And while I haven't ran any miles they've inspired me to start rising early in the morning and to start my own exercise program. Then it came to me while finishing my pushups one morning. **It is the life we live publicly that inspires people privately.** The prize for me is winning souls by the race I run. The prize has everything to do with simply running till the end. People are watching how you run, they're watching how you walk, talk, love your neighbors, forgive and even how you finish the race. They're wondering if you're going to hold out, stay the course, or give up and walk away. I'm not looking for wealth, houses, land; I'm looking for eternal life in Jesus Christ! I praise God that when I'm obedient to His Word I win and the prize is mine!

LIGHT BULB MOMENT:

Today the greatest prize is staying focused on my race and winning souls for the Kingdom of God. Remember you never know who's watching how you finish. Finish well. Have a great day.

_____
_____
_____
_____
_____
_____
_____
_____
_____
_____
_____
_____
_____
_____
_____
_____
_____
_____
_____
_____
_____
_____
_____
_____
_____
_____
_____
_____
_____

YOU'VE GOT TO HAVE THE WORD

No matter how far I go and how enormous the problems may seem in my life, there is one thing that always remains constant and powerful and that is the Word of God. Isn't it amazing how as believers we think we can go through our day without the Word? It's hard to wake up without thinking about Psalm 118:24 where it says, "This is the day the LORD has made; let us rejoice and be glad in it." Or when I face my enemies I can't help thinking about Psalm 23:4-5, "Even though I walk through the valley of the shadow of death, I will fear no evil, for you are with me; your rod and your staff, they comfort me. You prepare a table before me in the presence of my enemies. You anoint my head with oil; my cup overflows." And when I'm afraid he reminds me of David in Psalm 91, "He will cover you with his feathers, and under his wings you will find refuge; his faithfulness will be your shield and rampart."

It is the word of God that keeps me after everything else fails! God's word is constant, powerful, living and life changing. I'm so glad I'm a child of God and I realize that the Word is not only written on pages but in my heart! I praise God that the Word became flesh more than 2000 years ago so that I could live with power and authority. Thank you God for the Word and what it means to every believer when we speak it and apply it. AMEN!!!

LIGHT BULB MOMENT:

Make the Word a part of your week this week and share it with someone else. Find a key verse and meditate on it all week and watch your week become better.

_____
_____
_____
_____
_____
_____
_____
_____
_____
_____
_____
_____
_____
_____
_____
_____
_____
_____
_____
_____
_____
_____
_____
_____
_____

THE CHRISTMAS SPIRIT

I recently read a Facebook status that said, "I wish I could find the Christmas Spirit." It was the perfect beginning to my day because it reminded me what season I was in. I quickly reminded the Facebook fan that the spirit of Christmas was found more than 2000 years ago, in a barn, lying in a manger, wrapped in rags. He was the perfect gift that came to this world to free us, bless us and save man-kind. The wonderful thing is you don't have to search for Jesus, he's standing right there quietly waiting on us to call him. Acts 2:21 tells us, "And everyone who calls on the name of the Lord will be saved." Do you want to know a secret? Sometimes we're not in the right frame of mind to simply call on him. Depression and other mental illnesses often plague us during the most holy celebrations of the year. Why? Because the enemy wants us to forget the promise and fear our futures. But I rejoice in John 10:10 where Jesus says, "The thief comes only to steal and kill and destroy; **I have come that they may have life, and have it to the full."**

If you're searching for the Christmas spirit--it's already here! Luke 2:20 recaps the Shepherds visit to the stable where Christ was born. The bible says that the shepherds returned, glorifying and praising God for all the things they had heard and seen, which were just as they had been told.   As you enter this season of Christmas celebration, don't forget what you've seen or heard about Jesus Christ. Don't forget what he's already done for you. How he's blessed you to see another month. How he's blessed you to be alive. Don't wait for the gifts you'll receive this holiday season, celebrate the ultimate Gift

Jesus Christ. Remember what He's done for you year-round. Remember He is the reason for the season and much more.   Merry Christmas and a God Blessed New Year!!!!

LIGHT BULB MOMENT:

Think about all the gifts you've received in your life-time and ask yourself the question if any of them can truly compare to the gift of SALVATION?

_____
_____
_____
_____
_____
_____
_____
_____
_____
_____
_____
_____
_____
_____
_____
_____
_____
_____
_____
_____
_____
_____
_____
_____
_____

Week 32

I GOT WHAT I NEEDED

This Christmas season was different from all of the rest. My money was really funny and my change was definitely strange. Instead of trying to max out my credit cards and extend credit that couldn't budge any further, I found myself being content with what I had. You see in years past I've convinced myself that I really deserved all of the gifts and lavish holiday surprises. So I'd head to the store and make purchases beyond my budget and spend the remainder of the New Year wondering how I would pay the bills. And while I looked good and played the role I was financially and spiritually broken.

This year I decided that I could no longer say that Jesus was really the reason for the season. I had to live it and be content with the greatest gift of all--Jesus Christ! So I gave God his tithes first, paid my bills, put aside the credit cards and charge accounts. If I didn't have the cash I didn't make the purchase. I opened my house and surrounded myself with family and friends for the holidays and when I rested my head to go to sleep on Christmas night, I was in heavenly peace. Why? Because my focus was no longer on things and lavish gifts that I couldn't afford. My focus was on the joy that I was able to share with family and friends. My focus was on the New Year ahead and how I would move forward and conquer every challenge without the stress of Christmas debt. Things were no longer my god.

Joshua 24:15-16 reads, "Now fear the LORD and serve him with all faithfulness. Throw away the gods your forefathers worshiped beyond the River and in Egypt, and serve the LORD. But if serving the LORD seems undesirable to you, then choose for yourselves this day whom you will serve, whether the gods your forefathers served beyond the River, or the gods of the Amorites, in whose land you are living. But as for me and my household, we will serve the LORD." I thank God that I was able to put down the little gods of Christmas and pick-up the one true and living God of the universe. Have a blessed New Year.

LIGHT BULB MOMENT:

Are there any small gods living in your home or invading your life? Get rid of them and enjoy the God of the Universe 24/7.

_____
_____
_____
_____
_____
_____
_____
_____
_____
_____
_____
_____
_____
_____
_____
_____
_____
_____
_____

HE'S GOT HIS OWN PLAN

There are days when I find myself right in the middle of quick sand. It appears after all of the dancing, shouting and speaking in tongues that I wake up the next morning only to encounter trouble that tries to pull me down. I recently encountered a problem that gave me a little stress and right in the midst of praying hard for God to move--NOTHING happened. I woke up the next morning wondering what in the world have I done. I thought to myself, "I stepped out on faith God but you didn't catch me." A few days later God showed up and blew my mind. You see He didn't bless me the way that I expected! He did it His way. God had his own plan. It was better than I could have imagined. WOW!!!

Remember in Matthew 3:17 when Jesus was baptized? As soon as Jesus was baptized, He came up out of the water. At that moment heaven was opened, and He saw the Spirit of God descending like a dove and lighting on Him. Now watch this--immediately following this victorious event in the Kingdom of God, the next verse in Chapter 4 reads, "Then Jesus was led by the Spirit into the desert to be tempted by the devil."

God never told us that we wouldn't have trials and tribulations. He never told us that our trials would be delayed after we performed victorious service for Him. John 16:33 says "I have told you these things, so that in me you may have peace. In this world you will have trouble. But take heart! I have overcome the world." Now I thank God that he didn't bless me according to my plan, but He blessed me according to His plan! He didn't just look at my service to him, he simply did as any Father would and looked out for my best interest.

LIGHT BULB MOMENT:

Take the time to thank God for looking out for your best interest today. He could have blessed you your way but he took the time to do it his way. Thank you Jesus!

_____

_____

_____

_____

_____

_____

_____

_____

_____

_____

_____

_____

_____

_____

_____

_____

_____

_____

_____

_____

AN UNFAMILIAR PACKAGE

It never seems to fail--my blessings don't seem to come from the same old familiar places any longer. Just when I think it's coming from one direction, God does the ole switch-a-roo and sends it from another place. And while I am overjoyed at the outcome, I'm just a little puzzled that it didn't work my way. You see I thought I had it all planned. I prayed, fasted and told God what I needed and yes I kind of told him how to do His job. Sounds bossy huh? I know that's why I've asked God to forgive me.

You see I had an epiphany, I've been waiting on God to do a lot of things in my life. I've asked him to bless me in some miraculous ways. So I sit and wait and wait and wait, not realizing that God has already blessed me. The thing is it just didn't come in the package I was looking for. I asked God to help me be a better steward over my finances. I wanted God to show me how to save money. So I had to pay a large debt back within 12 months and wondered how I was going to do it. In December I looked back and realized I had paid off the debt and didn't lose a thing. I asked God why He allowed me to go through that challenging time. The Holy Spirit said, "I was teaching you how to save money." When I looked back at what I had done over the past 12 months I realized I could save more than $300 per month and still make ends meet. WOW!!!

Isaiah 55:8-9 reads, "For my thoughts are not your thoughts, neither are your ways my ways," declares the LORD." As the heavens are higher than the earth, so are my ways higher than your ways and my thoughts than your thoughts." I've decided to stop trying to figure God's way out and just follow His lead. After all, He knows best for all of us for He is God and it is He that made us and not we ourselves. **Stop looking for your blessings to arrive in the same old packages and prepare yourself for some out of the box miracles.**

LIGHT BULB MOMENT:

I like plastic bags, however I found out that paper was better for recycling. Regardless of what kind of package I like, they both get the job done. Remember God always gets the job done. When accepting His gift don't get caught up in the package!

_____
_____
_____
_____
_____
_____
_____
_____
_____
_____
_____
_____
_____
_____
_____
_____
_____
_____
_____
_____

UNLEARNING FEAR

Have you ever been afraid of something or someone? Ever found yourself frozen in fear and intimidated never wanting to confront a situation or a person? I have! It's amazing how fear can cripple or even bind you. That's why Paul told Timothy 25 times throughout the book of 2 Timothy not to be afraid. Over and over he encouraged him to be a bold soldier for Christ. You see, Timothy was a great follower, he was timid and loved the Lord and he also loved Paul dearly. Paul took him under his wing as a young disciple and prayed for him day and night, but there were times when Paul wasn't around that Timothy needed to take charge.

Paul was there when they laid hands on Timothy and he received the Holy Spirit. The prophecy over Timothy's life was that he would have awesome gifts of the Spirit to use in ministry. But Timothy was afraid to use his gifts. 2 Timothy 1:6 says, "Wherefore I put thee in remembrance that you stir up the gift of God that is in thee by the putting on of my hands". Paul reminded Timothy of his gifts and encouraged him to be bold and use them. He also spoke about fear in 2 Timothy 1:7 where it says, "For God hath not given us the spirit of fear; but of power, and of love, and of a sound mind."

When I remember that the spirit of fear doesn't come from God, I begin to think about all of the good things He does give me and one of those things is courage. Psychologists have discovered that we are born with only two fears falling and loud noises. The rest are learned. **So if I can learn a fear, I can unlearn it.** The comical thing is when I really examine the things and people I'm afraid of, I realize they're just things and humans and I no longer give them power over me. So I'm listening to Apostle Paul and remembering that there is nothing to be afraid of. Instead I choose to use my power, exercise my love and use my mind to serve my God.

LIGHT BULB MOMENT:

Take the time to write down some of your fears then begin to ask why. Now pray and ask God to remove those fears from you in the name of Jesus. Watch God begin to work wonders in your life. Have faith and believe.

_____
_____
_____
_____
_____
_____
_____
_____
_____
_____
_____
_____
_____
_____
_____
_____
_____
_____
_____
_____

HE KNOWS

Have you ever been in pain? I mean the kind of pain where you forget to pray and just begin to moan and groan. I recently experienced this kind of pain. It had me rocking to and fro grabbing my stomach. While speaking a long drawn out prayer wasn't my first thought but calling Jesus name was. Before I knew it I began to moan for relief. A short time later the pain began to subside. Now for those of you wondering why I didn't just go to the doctor, actually I did, but he instructed me that this pain was something I would have to deal with temporarily.

However in the midst of it, it felt like an eternity. After all my moaning and groaning the pain finally left. It was then that I remembered this scripture in Romans 8:26 where it says, "Likewise the Spirit also helpeth our infirmities: for we know not what we should pray for as we ought: but the Spirit itself maketh intercession for us with groanings which cannot be uttered." Isn't that awesome! I didn't know what to pray for neither did I have the strength, however the Holy Spirit did.

I'm so glad I serve a God who realizes that I have moments in my life when I fall apart and don't have the words to say. That's when He hears my heart and knows my every pain and desire. Just like a loving father He moves in and takes my pain away. Thank God for being my Father, my protector, my healer and my provider. God you're everything to me and much more.

LIGHT BULB MOMENT:

You may be able to remember a time when you were sick or you could be going through an illness right now. Remember God is a healer and He is the best medicine you could ever have!

_____
_____
_____
_____
_____
_____
_____
_____
_____
_____
_____
_____
_____
_____
_____
_____
_____
_____
_____
_____

Week 37

WHOSE SEASON IS IT?

I have often heard preachers and prophets alike tell people that it's their season. Proclaiming that this time in their life would bring great prosperity and blessings. However after reading Psalms 73 I'm reminded by the Psalmist Asaph that the wicked have a season of prosperity as well.

You see Asaph was King David's music director. He was also credited with putting much of the book of Psalms to music. Many folks may not know his name, however when you browse through the book of Psalms you'll find his name mentioned many times. Asaph was loyal to David and witnessed many triumphs, seasons of prosperity as well as tragedies that Israel suffered. He was there when King David died, witnessed Solomon's rise and his fall to idol Gods. He even witnessed the death of his family at the hands of Egyptians.

Asaph wrote the 73rd Psalm after his brother was murdered. Here is a portion of what he wrote in the New Living Translation, "What does God know? They ask. Does the most high even know what's happening? Look at these wicked people enjoying life of ease while their riches multiply. Did I keep my heart pure for nothing? Did I keep myself innocent for no reason? I get nothing but trouble all day long: every morning brings me pain. If I had really spoken this way to others, I would have been a traitor to your people. So I tried to understand why the wicked prosper. But what a difficult task it is! Then I went into your sanctuary, O God, and I finally understood the destiny of the wicked."

Asaph was troubled by the wicked reign which seemed to last an eternity. But when Asaph allowed himself to enter into the presence of the Lord and listened to His voice he found the answers that he needed and he realized that the wicked will not prosper but the righteous shall be victorious. Regardless of how hopeless you feel today, this is your season! Everyday belongs to us because we are the righteousness of God. Remember that God has not forgotten you and while the enemy rages, God will set them in slippery places and cast them down into destruction! **Pray for your enemies that they may see God before they fall.**

LIGHT BULB MOMENT:

I know you have some enemies as we all do. Take time today to pray for at least one of them and see if things don't begin to change in your life as well as theirs.

_____
_____
_____
_____
_____
_____
_____
_____
_____
_____
_____
_____
_____
_____
_____
_____

THE CREDIT'S NOT MINE

I recently read a review about an up and coming gospel music artist. The review disturbed me because it gave the artist credit for the moving of the Holy Spirit. It made me think about how many times I tried to take credit for something that happened and it was really God. You see, I had the audacity to think God needed me in order for things to happen. I forgot that He was just using my vessel to work through me. After all--He is God and He could just snap His finger and create someone else if He wanted to. God is bigger and mightier than anyone. The wonderful thing is that through His grace and mercy He continues to allow me to hang around Him.

Now I realize I have been anointed for His service, and as a vessel I can help to create an atmosphere for worship, but I can never take the credit for anything that God allows to happen. John 16:13 reads, "However, when He, the Spirit of truth, has come, He will guide you into all truth; for He will not speak on His own authority, but whatever He hears He will speak; and He will tell you things to come." Not even the Holy Spirit will try to exalt Himself or take credit for what He speaks, He gives the credit to God. One of the greatest things we can do in our daily walk with God is to give him the credit for every good and perfect thing that happens in our lives (James 1:17). For He is our creator and our sustainer.

LIGHT BULB MOMENT:

Take the time this week to think about some of the great
things you've done in life. Let your mind browse through
the compliments that others may have given you. Now take
a moment to think about who really deserved the credit.
Was it you or God working through you? I know the
answer--I just wanted to see if you did.

_____
_____
_____
_____
_____
_____
_____
_____
_____
_____
_____
_____
_____
_____
_____
_____
_____
_____
_____
_____

Week 39

UN-INHIBITED PRAISE

When I attended my daughter's graduation from high school, the weekend was filled with lots of emotion and plenty of joy. What a proud moment to see what God had truly done in our lives for the past 18 years. We expressed our joy through laughter, some spells of crying, loud shouts and some fancy dancing. Why? Because we were overjoyed with what God had done and the personal experiences we had with every trial and tribulation. We were not ashamed to show everyone just how joyful we were with what God had done. I embraced my graduate and loudly exclaimed to everyone around me, thank you Jesus, thank you Jesus! I didn't care where I was or who saw me, I know that it was because of Jesus that we were standing at my daughter's high school graduation with her 1st year of college already paid in full, additional scholarships and free admittance into a six week summer program. **My praise has no boundaries.**

David believed in celebrating before the Lord without any shame in 1 Samuel 6 chapter we find David bringing the Ark of the Covenant to his city. In 1 Samuel 6:20-22, we read this about David, "When David returned home to bless his own family, Michal, the daughter of Saul, came out to meet him. She said in disgust, "How distinguished the king of Israel looked today, shamelessly exposing himself to the servant girls like any vulgar person might do!" David retorted to Michal, "I was dancing before the LORD, who chose me above your father and all his family! He appointed me as the leader of Israel, the people of the LORD, so I celebrate before the LORD. Yes, and I am willing to look even more foolish than this, even to be

95

humiliated in my own eyes! 1 Samuel 6:23 informs us that Michal, the daughter of Saul, remained childless throughout her entire life.

Don't be ashamed to tell someone about God's goodness and the wonderful things He has done in your life. Don't be ashamed to shout it from the mountain-top! Do your dance! Romans 1:16 says, "For <u>I am not ashamed</u> of this Good News about Christ. It is the power of God at work, saving everyone who believes—the Jew first and also the Gentile." **Praise takes the chains off, praise will cause the barren to produce seed, praise will turn your dark days into days of sunshine.** Join me today as I proudly tell the world just how good God truly is.

LIGHT BULB MOMENT:

Take a moment each day this week to talk about God's goodness to strangers. Push yourself beyond the limits and express your adoration for Him. Watch the effect it has on others. You'll be blessed by their responses.

_____
_____
_____
_____
_____
_____
_____
_____
_____
_____
_____
_____

RAIN

One morning during a steady rain storm my attention shifted from my scripture reading to notice the rain that continuously fell on my deck. The more I concentrated on the rain I noticed that it went everywhere there was an opening. The rain quickly seeped into every nook and cranny. Those areas it couldn't get into it just covered them. That's how God is. When we yield to him – He comes in and saturates us with His presence and our lives are never the same. When we don't leave an opening for God, He just stands there waiting for the invitation. Never forcing Himself on us but gently waiting until we relinquish our will over to His.

That's the most difficult part--yielding. Paul talked about this in Romans 6:10 when he said, "I put this in human terms because you are weak in your natural selves. Just as you used to offer the parts of your body in slavery to impurity and to ever-increasing wickedness, so now offer them in slavery to righteousness leading to holiness." By yielding to God we become his slaves, his servants. That's when He can saturate us like the rain, clean us up and make us new again, and refresh us. When we refuse to yield and allow Him to have his perfect way in our lives we remain in a spiritual rut.

From now on when I see the rain, I'll ask myself the question, "Have I yielded to God today? Have I allowed Him to come in and do his perfect work in my life?" God saturate me now. Change me to be thy servant in Jesus name--AMEN.

LIGHT BULB MOMENT:

Take a glass of water and with your hands outstretched over the sink and your finger tightly fit together, pour the glass of water over them. Watch as the water fills every space and then slides gently through the spaces. Just like that water, allow God to saturate you more and more each day.

_____

_____

_____

_____

_____

_____

_____

_____

_____

_____

_____

_____

_____

_____

_____

_____

_____

_____

_____

SO YOU THINK YOU DESERVE MORE?

Do you ever think you deserve more from God? Perhaps you find yourself saying your prayers and running down your list of good things you've done for God and expecting him to do you a favor? I'm reminded of a story of a young man who had received a "C" in his PE class. He was really upset with the teacher. You see the teacher was also the football coach and most students didn't think he knew what he was doing in the classroom. So they didn't take his class seriously. He would often show films and have his students to complete work-sheets. There were no tests. So the young man decided to go to his teacher and inquire about the grade. When he asked the teacher why he received the "C", the teacher pulled out the grade book and began to show the young man all of the zeros he had received for not turning in his homework. When the teacher began to calculate the zeros and then average them out the grade was an "F". The teacher smiled and looked at the young man and said, "You're right, you don't deserve a "C" you deserve a "F". The young man then backed out of the room and told the teacher that's alright I got what I deserved.

We can never do enough good things to deserve God's goodness. I don't care how many "A's" you think you have, there are always some zeros in the grade book of life that will pull your spiritual average down. This is why I praise God for His grace and mercy; his unmerited favor that covers us and allows us to get "A's, B's and C's in life when we really deserve "F's". Ephesians 2:8 reads, "For it is by grace you have been saved, through faith—and this not from yourselves, it is the gift of God—." I thank God for His grace and mercy! I thank God that He doesn't use the grade book of life to hand out my blessings. I serve a God that looks past my faults and sees my needs every day. AMEN!!!!

LIGHT BULB MOMENT:

As a Christian what kind of grade do you think you deserve? Imagine if Jesus was handing out grades would you past the test?

_____
_____
_____
_____
_____
_____
_____
_____
_____
_____
_____
_____
_____
_____
_____
_____
_____
_____
_____
_____

Week 42

LIFE'S ALARM CLOCK

This devotion is really for the ladies – but it may help some brother to understand a little more about what we go through as women.

I recently turned 48 years old – yes ladies I'm telling my age. The birthday was met with a lot of excitement however 2 days prior to my birthday something began to happen to my health. It was like an alarm clock going off – and there wasn't a shut off button. It just got louder and louder. After two trips to the emergency room - I soon learned that it was pre-menopause!!! Yes I said it, the M word. You see all my life I had laughed at my mom, aunts and women in my family who went through what they called the change of life. But never in a million years did I expect to experience it as well. The toughest part for me was the mood swings and mind games that my internal clock played on me.

So when I went to the doctor for assistance I learned that my body was like a clock that needed to be reset and realigned with natural remedies but that wasn't all –I also realized my spiritual clock needed to be adjusted as well. That's when the Holy Spirit began to minister to me. So I began to adjust my time with God – instead of just studying and prayer time – I sought out a prayer partner someone who could cover me in prayer, and I added meditation time with God. Isaiah 26:3 reads "You will keep in perfect peace all who trust in you, all whose thoughts are fixed on you!

Today I feel great my physical clock is ticking better than ever and my spiritual clock is set for new experiences with

God. Pray for the women in your life who are experiencing life's changes, encourage them to embrace a life of healthy living and meditation with God.

Light Bulb Moment:

Make a list of individuals who you believe would make great prayer partners. I'll give you a hint – your list will not be long. Pray for those people and when the Holy Spirit leads you invite them for prayer time.

_____

_____

_____

_____

_____

_____

_____

_____

_____

_____

_____

_____

_____

_____

_____

_____

_____

_____

_____

Week 43

THIS IS HOW YOU DO IT

I had an opportunity to teach a class with young people on how to pray. I realized while they seem bored with ministry as usual, that if I taught them the best tools of Christianity they would understand the importance of a prayer life and that would draw them closer to God. The most amazing thing is watching them take the Word of God and using it in their prayers. Isaiah 55:11 describes this approach when it says, "So is my word that goes out from my mouth: It will not return to me empty, but will accomplish what I desire and achieve the purpose for which I sent it."

So I directed them to look at the challenges and needs in their lives and search the word of God for direction. For example: As a widow I needed God to help me with my finances. So I searched for every scripture I could find in the bible that dealt with widows and debt. As I searched the scriptures I quickly realized that those women had it worst than I did. Many were at their lowest points preparing to die with their children. You remember the widow at Zarephath who fed the prophet Elijah? So I read the stories, I read the trials and tribulations they faced, and I rejoiced in each of their victories.

Afterward my prayer said, "God help me to be as courageous as the widow at Zarephath and the widow who gave her last mite. Help me to have enough faith to listen and obey your voice. Help me to put you first and your ministry in the forefront of whatever I do. Send your divine direction as I prepare to rejoice in your blessings. God thank you for the blessings of more than enough. Thank you for sending abundance, thank you that there will be no lack in my life. In Jesus name I pray. Amen." Now what happened weeks following that prayer was amazing. God gave me insight, He gave me direction and He showed me favor in my finances. God taught me not to look at debt and money the same way. No I didn't hit the lottery, but I put things in the right place and God showed me favor. I thank God that His Word does not return back to Him void, and that whatever we ask God to do, He will do it. AMEN

LIGHT BULB MOMENT:

Begin to write down your prayer request to God, and find as many scriptures as you can that pertain to your request. After reading the scriptures, you will have a better understanding of how to direct your prayers. Now in your prayer time begin to rehearse God's Word back to Him, and watch God begin to move in your life like never before!

_____
_____
_____
_____
_____
_____
_____
_____
_____
_____
_____
_____
_____
_____

DOWNSIZING

When the New Year arrived I asked God to show me how to be a better steward over my finances. As always the Holy Spirit began to minister to me in ways I didn't quite expect. This is what he told me, "Eliminate excess." God wanted me to stop over-buying and to do away with the spirit of greed. "Reduce out-put." God wanted me to cut down on expensive over-head. If I didn't' need it I shouldn't buy it. Always look for a cheaper way to get it done. Lastly, "Pray about each purchase." Proverbs 3:6 instructs us to, "In all your ways acknowledge him, and he will direct your paths."

God is the best financial advisor you could ever have. He already has the investment plan and if you follow Him you will obtain all the wealth you will ever need. Moses took the time to remind the children of Israel in Deuteronomy 8:18 that it was God who gave them everything they had and more. It reads, "But remember the LORD your God, for it is he who gives you the ability to produce wealth, and so confirms his covenant, which he swore to your forefathers, as it is today." That same power rests, rules and abides with each believer today. We have the ability to be wealthy in every aspect of our lives, however we choose to allow the world to dictate how we obtain it. Embrace a life of wealthy living, become a tither, eliminate excess, reduce out-put, and pray about each purchase and I promise you that you will experience wealthy living. Have a great day!!!

LIGHT BULB MOMENT:

Make a list of things you purchase or pay for monthly that is unnecessary. Take the list and offer it up to God. Ask God to help you prioritize your spending. You will be surprised to find out what you need and what you don't need.

_____
_____
_____
_____
_____
_____
_____
_____
_____
_____
_____
_____
_____
_____
_____
_____
_____
_____
_____
_____
_____
_____
_____
_____
_____
_____

WORSHIP IS PART OF THE BREAKTHROUGH

I had a problem that I was seeking God's guidance for. After countless days and nights of praying I was left wondering what I needed to do next. That's when the Holy Spirit said, "Trust me and worship." At that point I began to worship God and tell Him how much I appreciated Him for listening and hearing my petition. But most of all I thanked Him for being God. You see without God there would be no me, no good or bad. Without God I wouldn't be able to live, move or experience life to the fullest.

John 1:3 reads, "Through him all things were made; without Him nothing was made that has been made." I must recognize God with my worship. I must acknowledge Him with my thanks. I must praise Him with my trust. Worship is part of your breakthrough! It holds the key to a life of everlasting fulfillment. Without it there is no intimacy with God. King David was a worshipper. David realized no matter how angry he became and frustrated over his circumstances, that it was the worship that would take him into his place of breakthrough. Listen to what happened with David after his child died, "Then David got up from the ground, washed himself, put on lotions, and changed his clothes. He went to the Tabernacle and worshiped the LORD. After that, he returned to the palace and was served food and ate."

I don't know what your problem may be today, but just remember that **after you've prayed a while worship will get you through it!**

LIGHT BULB MOMENT:

Take the time this week to worship God on your own time. Use your devotion time to worship God and see what happens.

_____
_____
_____
_____
_____
_____
_____
_____
_____
_____
_____
_____
_____
_____
_____
_____
_____
_____
_____
_____
_____
_____

I REFUSE TO GO DOWN

Have you ever had someone try to wear you down, constantly mistreating you and trying to break your spirit? Perhaps you have a boss, family member or even a church member who never seems to give you a break. That's what happened to the children of Israel. The Egyptians tried to wear them down. They forced them into slavery and mistreated them. However instead of the Hebrews giving up; they multiplied and grew stronger! I guess you could say that they were Be'be's kids.

When we are burdened and overwhelmed with problems, that's not the time to give up, that's the time to raise up and lift your head! At your lowest point remember the children of Israel. They had reached their pit, but they decided to make the best of it instead of wallowing in it. Exodus 1:12 reads, "But the more the Egyptians oppressed them the more the Israelites multiplied and spread, and the more alarmed the Egyptians became." **Remember you can't be an over-comer without troubles and you can't get stronger without a work-out!** Join me this week as we overwhelm the enemy and cause him to flee. James 4:7 reads "Submit yourselves, then, to God. Resist the devil, and he will flee from you."

LIGHT BULB MOMENT:

Look at a problem you have. Ask yourself these questions: Where did it come from? Why is it happening? Is there something you can do to fix it? If you have no control over the problem then give it to the problem solver. Visualize yourself handing it over to God and watch the burden lighten. When God tells you to move get ready to move. Amen!!!

_____
_____
_____
_____
_____
_____
_____
_____
_____
_____
_____
_____
_____
_____
_____
_____
_____
_____
_____
_____
_____
_____
_____
_____
_____

SPECIAL SKILLS

It always amazes me how God will give you a gift and allow you to use it for His glory. I love watching people who can sing, dance and even preach use their talents for God. However there are many people who attend church Sunday after Sunday and never use the gifts that God has given them to support the body of Christ. I was reading Exodus 28:3 the other day and this is what it said, "Instruct all the skilled craftsmen whom I have filled with the spirit of wisdom. Have them make garments for Aaron that will distinguish him as a priest set apart for my service." God gifted the men to sew Aaron's priestly garments. They were given wisdom by God in order to do their task. Every tassel, every piece of trim, every stitch was guided by God.

I realize your gift may not take you before large crowds and even receive a thunderous applause, but remember God is watching and cheering you on from the heavenly stands! Think about your special talents and abilities. You may be able to sew, paint, draw, repair cars, clean, cook or simply make phone calls. Whatever your God-given gift is, use it to the fullest. Focus on how you can use your gift in the body to help others. As you commit this to God, He will give you the wisdom to use His gifts and allow you to accomplish the task.

LIGHT BULB MOMENT:

Make a list of your gifts. Ask yourself this question, "Are you using them for God's glory?" If not ask God to show you how to use your gifts for the up-building of his Kingdom.

_____
_____
_____
_____
_____
_____
_____
_____
_____
_____
_____
_____
_____
_____
_____
_____
_____
_____
_____
_____
_____

HIS EYES HAVE COMPASSION

There are times in our lives when we feel that we are going through our troubles all alone. It seems like no one is there or even notices the struggles that we're having. No one calls or even inquires about us. That's how Job felt. Job referred to God as a watcher or observer of humanity. He felt like God was his enemy just sitting back watching him go through. This is what he said in Job 7:20 "If I have sinned, what have I done to you O watcher of all humanity? Why make me your target? Am I a burden to you?"

We must remember that God watches us, but with eyes of compassion. He sees our every trial and tribulation as a father who loves us with eyes of protection. It is during those lonely times that God is behind the scenes orchestrating the good that will eventually come out of our struggles. At your lowest point He's building you up to stand. When the weight seems too heavy, God pushes you through the pain of the burdens, and then just like that He takes the burden on his shoulders. Why? Because God knows just how much you can bear. Remember you are never alone. It's the quietness during the struggle that makes it seem that you're alone. But always remember that God is quietly sitting in the corner preparing for your rescue.

LIGHT BULB MOMENT:

Ask yourself this question this week, "Has God rescued me lately?"

_____
_____
_____
_____
_____
_____
_____
_____
_____
_____
_____
_____
_____
_____
_____
_____
_____
_____
_____
_____
_____
_____
_____

IT'S FOR YOUR GOOD

Remember when your parents used to put you on punishment? They had all kinds of tactics, the spankings, time-out, restriction, going to bed early, extra chores. You name it and our parents tried it. They were very crafty in their punishments indeed. The most difficult thing was trying to understand as an 8 year old how spanking me with a belt was for my own good. Especially when it hurt so bad but of course years later I understood the lessons behind all those spankings. They taught me there were negative consequences for my negative actions. They taught me discipline was a part of my growth and of course that disobedience hurts.

All those were such important lessons that rest with me today. I've even passed those life lessons down to my children and I know that they will pass them on to theirs. Hebrews 12:6-7 reads, "Because the Lord disciplines those he loves, and He punishes everyone He accepts as a son. Endure hardship as discipline; God is treating you as sons. For what son is not disciplined by his father?" When I endure discipline by God it is a reminder that He loves me and wants me to obey His word. It is also a reminder that He sees the good in me and wants it to come forth. Many of my struggles come from my disobedience and therefore I must remember what the writer of Hebrews 12:5-6 says, "My son, do not make light of the Lord's discipline, and do not lose heart when He rebukes you, If you are not disciplined then you are illegitimate children and not true sons." Thank you God for the discipline you hand out and while I don't like it, I realize it is a reminder that I am your child.

LIGHT BULB MOMENT:

When was the last time you were disciplined by God? Take this week to think about how merciful God was and how the punishment could have been even worse.

_____
_____
_____
_____
_____
_____
_____
_____
_____
_____
_____
_____
_____
_____
_____
_____
_____
_____
_____
_____
_____

A CHANGE

I recently turned 48 years old. Yes ladies--I'm telling my age. That's not what disturbs me the most. I didn't realize that after all these years things would begin to change so quickly. I got sick, experienced hot flashes, mood swings and yes even some panic attacks. I asked God during my devotion time, why He allowed my internal alarm clock to go off with such a bang. I couldn't understand why I had to go through these changes. I know women who don't experience anything quite like the changes that I was experiencing.

The Holy Spirit whispered softly to me that every living creature has seasons. He said, "Prepare yourself Linda for a new season in your life both physically and spiritually." Then he took me to Ecclesiastes 3:1 where it says, "There is a time for everything, and a season for every activity under heaven…" I smiled when I heard His voice so clearly. **I realized that my greatest pain came from my struggle with the change.** So I've decided to embrace it. I've decided to fan when I'm hot, pray when I hurt and take care of my temple the way God intended. And while I'm embracing the physical change God will be working on the spiritual change in my life. My anointing will grow stronger, my gifts will grow and my faith will intensify. Thank God for the changes of life and never leaving me as I go through them.

LIGHT BULB MOMENT:

What changes have you made this year? How did they impact your life? How did they help you to grow spiritually? Praise God for the changes!

_____
_____
_____
_____
_____
_____
_____
_____
_____
_____
_____
_____
_____
_____
_____
_____
_____
_____
_____
_____
_____
_____
_____
_____
_____
_____

HE KNEW ME

I find myself daily trying to balance things in my life. I work hard to give God my time, energy and resources. I strive to spend valuable time with my children and family and of course to remain committed to my earthly job. And last but not least, making sure I have carved out some time just for me. So I use early mornings as my time of devotion, reflection, or to simply think about me. The thing that keeps a smile on my face is that every time I try to think about me, I end up thinking about God.

You see I can't just focus on me because I keep seeing God's hand in everything I do and at every turn of my life. When I was born He was there, when I was sick He was there. During my greatest moments He was there. In my struggles He was there. Jeremiah said it best in Jeremiah 1:5, "Before I formed you in the womb I knew you, before you were born I set you apart;" The Hebrew word for knew is "Yada". This word has many meanings, however in this passage it means: Understanding the needs of those around us and taking care of them. God understood our needs before we were born and He already made provision to take care of them.

So the next time I feel overwhelmed, underappreciated or all alone in this big complex world; I'll remember "Yada". I will remember the fact that God has always been there looking out for me--even when I didn't know him.

LIGHT BULB MOMENT:

Remember this week that YOU are truly special. God made provisions for you before you were born.

_____
_____
_____
_____
_____
_____
_____
_____
_____
_____
_____
_____
_____
_____
_____
_____
_____
_____
_____
_____
_____
_____
_____
_____
_____
_____

A LIFE WITH INTERRUPTIONS

I lost one of my dear friends. She was a beautiful woman, a single mother and a believer in Jesus Christ. She was a joy to be around because she always brought laughter into our conversations when we were together. I'll miss that lazy laugh and her stylish ways. She died after struggling for more than a year with cancer.

I often think about her and while studying my devotion one morning I ran across the scripture that reminded me of her Eulogy. Isaiah 43:1-2 reads, "But now thus saith the Lord that created thee, O Jacob, and he that formed thee, O Israel, Fear not; for I have redeemed thee, I have called thee by thy name; thou art mine. When thou passeth through the waters, I will be with thee; and through the rivers, they shall not overflow thee; when thou walkest through the fire, thou shalt not be burned; neither shall the flame kindle upon thee."

While her life was filled with divine interruptions God redeemed her. **He traded in her life of struggles for a crown of life in the heavens.** And regardless of what interruptions came her way, she was never overtaken by the waters, she was never consumed by the fire of sickness, she simply reached her destination with Jesus. I no longer say that I lost her, I am proud to say that she is resting with Jesus Christ.

LIGHT BULB MOMENT:

Remember death is a definite part of life, but to know Jesus means an eternal life with Him.

_____
_____
_____
_____
_____
_____
_____
_____
_____
_____
_____
_____
_____
_____
_____
_____
_____
_____
_____
_____
_____
_____
_____
_____

I end this devotional book with much praise and thanksgiving. This was a divine push from on High. There were days I didn't want to write, but God reminded me of who He was and what He had put in me needed to be shared with others. Thank God for the victories in our lives.

-The End-

By the Word

Word

MOMENTS

A Devotional Guide